Gifts & Secrets

Life and Love Lessons from a Real Mom

Gifts & Secrets

Life and Love Lessons from a Real Mom

Kim Sorensen

Carpenter's Son Publishing

Gifts & Secrets: Life and Love Lessons from a Real Mom

© 2021 by Kim Sorensen

Published by Carpenter's Son Publishing, Franklin, Tennessee

Published in association with Larry Carpenter of Christian Book Services, LLC

www.christianbookservices.com

Cover design by Suzanne Lawing

Interior design by Adept Content Solutions

Printed in the United States of America

978-1-952025-70-9

Parents can only give good advice

or put them on the right paths,

but the final forming of a person's character

lies in their own hands.

—Anne Frank

D ear Reader,
Life is messy. We all wish that when they handed us our bundle of joy, they came with a manual on how to not mess them up. Since children don't come with instructions, I decided to create a simple book with life lessons that helped me and my husband create a framework to raise our boys to be kind, confident, and respectful. Isn't that what we all want as parents?

My life and parenting experiences were not perfect. When I began this book journey, it was destined to be a cherished single copy keepsake for my boys. A collection of the successes they grew up through that they could share with their own children. During the journey of creating this keepsake, I was encouraged to share these lessons with others, in hopes of bringing a sense of ease and simplicity to one of the most rewarding and yet hardest jobs on earth, parenthood. This book is the tangible result of this mom's messy soul seeking to pass on to my own children the intangible essence of loving and living with simple life lessons. Now I pass these things along to you as well.

I am just a regular mom with a heart that hopes this inspires you and your family to see how instilling gratitude and goodness into the hearts of your family is manageable without big elaborate and time-consuming drama. Your success as a parent isn't based on if you follow the suggestions in this book or by how many parenting books you have read. It is determined by the love and trust your children have for you and the bridges that you build to keep the communication going even in the roughest of years. Don't let yourself be discouraged by someone's social media highlight reel. We all struggle through the years as we learn and grow alongside our children. What your highlight reel looks like doesn't matter, what matters is the heart and soul, the time and talent, and the investment of yourself into the little people God has entrusted you to care for.

You don't need money and fame to define who you are or how you raise your children. I am not wealthy, nor was I wealthy growing up. The things that we provided for our boys came with sacrifice and long-term planning. **Provision is a decision** and we all can make different choices when we are dedicated to a specific goal. Whether that goal is saving for a memorable vacation or preparing to buy a car for a new teen driver, we know that thinking forward makes all the difference in reaching those goals.

Take your time reading each chapter and think about each question when you reach the end. Be inspired to create a safe place for your children to grow up with your own lessons, traditions, and experiences.

When you do this, you will have your own *Gifts and Secrets* stashed away in your heart, you will always be rich.

Cheers!

Contents

Introduction

Leaving a Legacy

What kind of legacy do you want to leave? As the youngest of six children (four brothers and a sister), making my mark on the world was always harder, knowing someone else had already done it before me. When there are no magical firsts that a sibling didn't conquer before you, you begin to wonder how to set yourself apart. Luckily for me, I was raised in a family that made sure everyone knew they mattered. We grew up in a town where everyone knew everyone, and the streets were safe. My parents were blue-collar workers and, while we didn't have a ton of money, any deficiency was made up with tons of practical advice and direction on ways to make memories.

Family was everything to my parents. When I think about their impact on my life it brings on a flood of memories and moments where they made sure we always knew we were important, valued, and loved. It inspired me to leave my own thumbprint on the tree of traditions my parents had planted in us. It was a bountiful planting scattered over six kids, spouses, twenty grandchildren, and seven great grandchildren. How do you make your mark on the world? For me, it all began when I became a mother. The gratitude I have for all the lessons my parents taught me now had a deeper purpose. I knew I wanted to take everything my parents had shown me and instill it within the boys I had been entrusted with. You and I both know that is easier said than done.

While we all may have shared similar lessons, our experiences are just as unique as our fingerprints. As a mom, simple was always the name of the game. Through simple activities, lessons, and, of course leading by example, I strived to create and leave my sons a legacy that they could pass on to their own children. This book, and the lessons it contains, is part of that legacy.

I know what you're thinking: *I don't need another parenting book.* While none of these ideas are new or original, the experiences from them are uniquely mine. Why are lessons that others learn so important? They help us to reduce the time it takes for us to learn them. The hard lessons that my parents learned passed on to me a compressed version of those lessons so that I could reduce the pain I would go through and get to my destination faster. That is what this book is. It isn't a perfect roadmap for parenthood. It is a collection of experiences that I pray will help you to bypass some of the time it takes learning them yourself.

As a full-time mom, it was always my intention to do the best I could. Each priceless moment I share with you is from my heart. No one is a bigger expert on their lives and how lessons have impacted them than we are. I don't know what you have been through and I don't claim to have all the answers. What I do know is that I am the expert at raising up my own family.

Through my life lessons, mistakes, failures, and successes, no one knows more than I do how to reach the other side of the obstacles that I have faced. This is my short-cut guide. Inspired by my amazing parents, by motherhood to three now successful boys, and of course, my husband who has journeyed this life with me and helped me cut the path in the uncharted territories of our lives. This guide is meant to give you a chance to avoid some of the pain that life has to offer, while creating memories to last a lifetime.

Come with me on a journey to laugh, pause, learn, and most importantly, to see how love and committing yourself to be present with those you have been entrusted with can change the world. Not just yours, but theirs. We know that God gives each of us a purpose. Part of mine was motherhood and raising my family. Our purpose may not be the same, but our God is. He told us, "Train up a child in the way he should go, and when he is old he will not depart from it" (Prov. 22:6 NKJV).

Are you ready?

CHAPTER 1

The Gift of a Father's Advice

There is a little known fact about life and the world. It's a fact that many of us are not fond of, but one we can at least all agree on: Life isn't fair. Not only is it not fair, but life doesn't owe any of us a thing. As parents, we work hard to instill these truths while fighting against them. Health problems, car accidents, injuries, and death are all things that hit us at some point in our lives and in our parenting journey. Explaining that life isn't fair while hating the unfairness of it is very real, and it is a feeling we must make sure our children understand.

You see, all children must look after their own upbringing, but parents are the first and most important

1

teachers that set them on the path of *character*. It can be easy as a parent to blame things on circumstance and bad days, but we each have a responsibility to our own behavior, and we have to remember a few standard rules.

My father was a pro at giving advice that I still refer to every day. These lessons helped me parent my own kids. The information isn't new, but because my dad made sure it was always in the front of our minds growing up, I made sure it was on the top of my kids' minds too. It hasn't failed me yet.

When my day heads south from good to bad, I walk through those lessons my dad gave me. These were his rules.

1. The world is not fair.

2. Everyone has a boss.

3. Living involves hassle.

4. Nobody is entitled to anything.

5. Pride is self-respect and must be earned, not given.

6. Being loved is free only for babies; after that stage of life, reciprocity is required.

7. Everybody goofs a lot.

8. Everybody is laughable.

9. Staying happy involves work.

I can sense you wincing at how cliché all of those rules are. Think about how much truth is in each one. If you stopped for a moment and instead of reacting to a problem, first stood that problem up against which rule applies, how would it change your reaction? Let me share an example of a time I applied my father's advice to my boys:

Boys will fight. There are more times than I can count where my three boys would taunt one another until mayhem ensued and usually something got broken. One such time provided the perfect opportunity to teach them about a little thing called, *guilty by association*. I could hear the fighting from the other room, two distinct voices arguing over who got to sit in a specific chair. As their voices got louder, I heard one of them call out, "Quack, quack!" Since neither of my three boys was a duck, a shoving match began. Before anyone knew it, the chair was shoved through the glass door of my china cabinet.

Unfortunately for my other son, he was about to learn this lesson the hardest. While he didn't participate in the aggression that resulted in the damage, he *did* stand there watching. This was a moment where I chose to discipline all three for their acts. Two for obviously fighting, and the third for doing nothing. Some parents may think it seems odd to punish a child for doing nothing; however, what if he came and got either myself or his father before it escalated? Or what if he had chosen to stop the fight himself?

If he had chosen one of those two paths, nothing would have been broken.

Even as adults, we often find ourselves wondering if it's worth it to do the right thing. We try to weigh it in our minds and choose the best course of action but choosing right over choosing to do nothing will *always* be the best choice. I knew that by teaching them this fact, my boys would learn how to be more proactive, to help step in when it was needed, and by doing so, tilting the world in their favor.

Do you remember a time when you should have stepped in? Do you think things would be different if you hadn't sat on the sidelines remaining uninvolved? As parents, we not only get a chance to take all the lessons, good and bad, that we learned from our parents and put them into practice, but we also get to expand on those lessons and create versions of our own.

What advice can you implement from your parents to lend to your legacy?

_____

_____

_____

_____

_____

Your Notes

_____

_____

_____

_____

_____

_____

_____

_____

_____

_____

_____

_____

_____

_____

_____

_____

_____

_____

_____

_____

_____

CHAPTER 2

The Career of Motherhood

Motherhood is a rough career. It comes with long hours, very little recognition, and the worst part is how many people believe that being a mother is the easiest job in the world! Many people think full-time moms live incredible days filled with soap operas and laziness. Perhaps you think stay-at-home moms have it easy. Maybe you are a stay-at-home mom and you have been placed in this stereotypical box before. Women tend to be the first to tear each other down, and men who have been working long hours wonder how so little gets done throughout the day.

The truth of motherhood is that every day comes with challenges and issues that we can't foresee.

Chances are if you get home and your spouse hasn't gotten the things you *think* should be done, you might want to do a mental and verbal check-in to find out how the day actually went. You might be surprised to find out that someone got sick, hurt, or maybe your spouse was just overwhelmed. Stay at home moms or dads have a job that, until you have lived it, you just can't claim to understand.

Despite my business degree and professional qualifications, motherhood brought with it many qualifications I had to learn as I went. I was blessed to have the flexibility to make motherhood a full-time job. Not only did I have the opportunity to raise my boys full-time, my husband and I had the joy of being the billet (home) for our local hockey team. We invited seven junior players into our homes to be a part of our family during the hockey season. Putting yourself in a position to mother other children is an experience like no other, and to this day we are in contact with most of them.

Another incredible experience we had throughout raising our family was being short-term foster parents. Through a program called Cradle Care (or "interim/ transitional care"), we were screened and approved to provide a loving family to care for infants whose adoption plans are still being finalized. Those chosen to care for your baby are called "Cradle Care families" and it was an honor and a privilege to be a part of a child's journey to becoming part of their new family.

It made it so much more powerful as a mom to see that transition happening for a family and a child. There are no words to describe every child that we placed in the arms of the family that had eagerly been waiting, sometimes for many years, to finally meet their new son or daughter. It was a special time in our family's life and I know it is something that taught my boys the value of family.

Motherhood Comes in Stages

In my career of motherhood, there are three "promotions."

For me, it began when those double lines showed up on the pregnancy test. Something many men struggle to understand is the immediate change that happens in their significant other when they realize they are going to be a mom. It may be a nine-month journey to seeing that baby, but the heart and soul know immediately. It is a change that no event that comes after can alter. The title of *mother* only grows from that moment forward, and it comes with two more promotions.

As your child grows, you watch them go through their own relationship struggles. At some point in their adulthood you will have someone else to call daughter or son. This change comes in the form of the joy, and sometimes the challenges, of the partners with whom your children choose to share their lives and their love. Gaining another beloved son or daughter in your child's spouse can come as a wonderful surprise.

Having someone new in the family means that you may find some cultural or religious differences. Sometimes, conflict with the future spouse—and even their family—may rise. It is inevitable when two different families combine. The values, rules, and lifestyles may be on opposite sides of each other. The "two becoming one" is not only for those that exchange the vows but also for the extended families involved.

The third and even more wonderful promotion comes in the gift of grandchildren. What a beautiful moment when your children's children snuggle up next to you and say, "I love you, Mimi" (or Nana, Grams, or Grandma).

I already have the bookshelf for my future grandchildren, made by my three boys. This bookshelf has begun collecting the books that I will read with the "Littles" on my lap. Just as I had done with their daddies. There is nothing that creates a connection with those you love more than making time to do the things that will create a lasting impact. I can say from experience that the time I spent reading to my boys is priceless and it has created a lasting impression on each of them, even when they grew out of it.

It is worth repeating: In our household the lessons began when my sons were very young. As I found teachable moments, I took advantage of them. The most amazing thing about being present in your children's life into adulthood is that those teachable moments continue to present themselves even now that they are adults. In the beginning they were lessons, and as the boys grew in age the lessons morphed into "The Rules." Those rules have given them a foundation to rely on and to build lives of integrity as they create their own families.

How, as a mother or father, are you leaving a legacy with your family?

_____

_____

_____

_____

_____

_____

_____

_____

_____

_____

_____

_____

_____

_____

_____

_____

_____

_____

_____

_____

_____

_____

_____

_____

_____

_____

_____

_____

_____

_____

CHAPTER 3

The ABCs: Actions, Behaviors, Consequences

Teaching memorable lessons that leave an impact on your children requires two things: consistency and repetition. Repetition can take the form of visible reminders. It also helps if you can find a memorable way to convey the lesson. For us, the way we reminded our sons was with the ABCs of life. They were displayed on our refrigerator with alphabet magnets we used to teach them their ABCs.

The primary lesson I taught my children was that Actions lead to Behaviors, which result in Consequences. As my sons grew up, there were many opportunities to illustrate this lesson, as it pertained to mistakes as well as the good consequences of right actions and behaviors. This is where rules come in. Rules are important because they create guidelines for our children to make decisions without the excessive freedom that can lead to disastrous behaviors. Newton's Law shows us *for every action there is an equal* (in size) *and opposite* (in direction) *reaction.* The goal is to give them the space to learn safely until they gain the wisdom and foresight to realize these things on their own.

As your children build relationships with friends and begin to mature, there will be times when the impact of their friends' decisions will affect everyone. Disagreements among friends will happen—none of us escape the occasional argument or disagreement, even with our closest friends. It is how we deal with those moments of conflict that can determine how much grace and love we have for each other. As teenagers, it can be the toughest time when we find ourselves in a position of leadership over a friend who has hurt us.

There was a time in those tumultuous teenage years that this exact thing played itself out in our family. One of our son's friends had a managerial position and worked with another friend from the group of kids our son hung out with. One angry fight later, that manager decided to turn in their friend for breaking a rule they had broken themselves. Anger is a nasty thing that discolors everything we see and distances us from the sanity needed to process a fight without creating more conflict and division. Since they acted out of emotion, their friend lost his job. It goes from just affecting the two parties in the fight to impacting the entire group of friends because all of the families involved are so close. It also puts the friends not involved in a position to choose sides.

The "Joy" of Driving with Kids

Luckily, raising boys means that I was given many teachable moments to show our sons about those ABCs of life. One of the funniest examples we had is when my husband was driving the boys to school one day. If you have ever driven children in your car, you know that there are times when you just can't handle the fighting and arguing anymore. This was one of those times.

Two of the boys were arguing about something that was forgotten even in the midst of the argument. My husband had more than enough and asked them to please stop. Every parent can agree that there will be more times than you have fingers and toes where your kids will be completely oblivious to your requests for peace. This was no different. With no one listening to him, he pulled over and demanded that all three get out and walk the rest of the way to school. Sometimes it takes extreme measures to make your point. Sadly, they missed the first part.

My husband proceeded to drive away and called me to let me know what happened. I called the school and shared that the boys would be late. I wish I could say they decided that since they had been left to walk to school, they needed to change their attitudes. Instead, the two that were having a disagreement in the car began having an all-out brawl in the yard of a local business.

Being Heard

Shortly after, I received a call from a family friend, who worked for the police department. Someone had called in to report that there was a problem and he had been dispatched to check it out. When he arrived, they were still duking it out and he called to let me know that while it wasn't supposed to be funny, he got a good chuckle out of the situation. I asked what he thought should happen next, and he said, "Best that they get on to school." The youngest, who had nothing to do with the whole situation, had already made it to school, leaving them behind to finish their nonsense alone. I had to call my husband to break up the sibling love of beating each other senseless. When the other two made it to school late, they were greeted by the principal with grass stains on their khaki pants and white polos.

Despite the chaos that comes with parenting, they hear more than we think they do. To my surprise, one of my sons shared this with me: "We learn from a very young age that we are going to do things both good and bad again and again. It all starts when we were learning how to walk. When I started learning to walk, I must have tried standing only to fall instantly more times than you could probably count, Mom. But soon I was walking. When we are kids, we are going to keep trying something until we learn how to do it. Having rules is important because they restrict the action that can lead to disastrous consequences or right actions and behaviors." When he shared this with me, I admit, it was a moment that I had been waiting for. They are listening, you just have to be willing to repeat the rules and help your children commit those lessons and teachable moments to their memory. Not just for the moment, but for a lifetime.

What ABC's of life can you share with your children that you have learned from?

_____

_____

_____

_____

_____

_____

_____

_____

_____

_____

_____

_____

_____

_____

_____

_____

_____

_____

_____

_____

_____

_____

_____

_____

_____

_____

_____

_____

_____

_____

_____

_____

_____

_____

_____

_____

_____

_____

_____

_____

_____

_____

_____

_____

_____

_____

_____

_____

_____

_____

_____

CHAPTER 4

Scouts

When we build a strong foundation at home, it is something we can see in the public space as well. There are many organizations that help create that sense of integrity and humanity in our children. Those places also begin to build the patterns of behavior and respect that apply to society as well. Responsibility is something that our children will learn in all places of life. For us, we knew we wanted our boys to be involved in something that would help them learn more than just school knowledge. Life skills are priceless.

Scouts, and other organizations like it, are increasingly important because our young people are no longer learning basic life skills. Scouting also prepares kids to deal with the unexpected things in life. Both my husband and I were involved in our sons' Scouting careers from Cubs to Eagle. I think my husband learned many life lessons while we journeyed through this time with our boys. I know I did.

Take the camping weekends for instance. They would make up a duty roster assigning each member an assignment for the weekend. That assignment would be in the area of menu planning, equipment needs, and setting up camp. They would prepare a list of clothing they would need for overnight campouts in either warm or cold weather. Packing for each camping trip instilled new lessons, like when cold camping trips were being packed for, they needed to understand the importance of layers.

One of my favorite Scout lessons was *leave no trace*, which was a fancy way of telling the boys that they couldn't interrupt nature. To translate, it meant cleaning up after oneself. It was very important to me for them to learn the skills of focus and hard work early on, especially in advance of the high school distractions like sports, clubs, relationships, and cars that I knew they would encounter in high school.

The commitment that they made to being in Scouts meant there were many missed weekends hanging out with friends that weren't in Scouts when Scout camping trips came up. For me, with how quickly technology advanced once I was parenting teenagers, it motivated me to create a rule that helped our boys keep their commitment to finishing Scouts. It also put us in a position to help them learn real responsibility before handing them the biggest life distraction: cell phones. Our boys weren't allowed cell phones until they became Eagle Scouts, which each of the three achieved by the age of fourteen. It wasn't easy, but they were committed and each saw the reward, not only in the cell phone, but in the lessons learned throughout each Scout adventure.

Those adventures were many and I can say that it was mostly my husband who took the boys on all of their camping trips. No doubt he treasures the experiences of fun and has moments that are bittersweet mixed with a little agony. From the time that they were in Cub Scouts until they achieved the rank of Eagle Scout, the boys would go on many campouts all through the year in all kinds of weather. A slightly larger age gap meant my youngest was in a different group of Scouts, so we had the privilege of being part of twice as many Scouting events.

One such campout was during a cold snap, when my middle son needed a two-mile hike to qualify for a merit badge. To make sure that he was not alone for such a tough badge, his brother joined in, and two other boys made two-mile brisk hike together. If you can imagine a two-mile hike in the briskest of weather, it was a balmy 19°F with a wind chill of -10°F!

Windy Lessons

Another Scouts memory that bears mentioning was a three-day campout with multiple troops featuring a midnight storm. It came with all the best storm accessories including high winds, inches of rain, and storm shelter alarms. As everyone rushed to the shelter, both of my sons and husband took the time to make sure their tent fly was secure before joining the others. Once the whole camp assembled in the shelter, a head count was made and one of the other troops was missing someone. Three of the troop leaders braved the wind and rain and found him next to a tree, soaked to the bone, and (thankfully) not too far away enabling them to get back to the safety of the storm shelter. After an hour or so, the storm subsided, and everyone went back to their camps. Stepping out of the storm shelter revealed water and tree branches everywhere.

The damage to camp was worse than expected. Most of the tents were blown wide open. Scattered everywhere were waterlogged sleeping bags and muddy clothing strewn every which way. That is, all the tents except my sons' and my husband's 2 tents. Those few extra moments they took meant everything was dry as a bone inside their tents.

My husband and sons shared their dry clothing and sleeping bags with the other boys and leaders. I swell with pride when I think of this moment because, how often do we respond to crisis in a manner that is halfhearted? Through the lessons they had learned up to this moment, they knew to be prepared. Those fifteen seconds to secure their things meant, not only were their things dry and safe, but they had supplies to share with those who had fled in the onset of the chaos.

On each one of my sons' campouts, some lessons were learned that would make a difference in their lives later on. Even though many of these campouts were only a few miles from our home, they learned how to deal with each problem that came up and needed an answer before they could move on.

While I wasn't in the trenches of every camping trip, I did have the chance to help my sons with their annual popcorn sales. That meant we worked together to organize a solution to selling all their allotted popcorn (as well as some extra). Those life lessons we learned through camping trips and sales gave them a solid foundation in survival, problem solving, communication, and how to sell. As life would have it, those lessons in popcorn sales found two of my sons building their careers in sales. All the lessons that we have the chance to instill will bring your children fruit in their lives, as long as you take the chance to seize those teachable moments.

More than hard work, this basic framework helped them learn early on how creating a goal and making sacrifices create the path that allows the goal to be achieved quicker than anyone can imagine.

Share some important reasons why joining an organization is good for character-building and goal-setting.

_____

_____

_____

_____

_____

_____

_____

_____

_____

_____

_____

_____

_____

_____

_____

_____

_____

Your Notes

_____

_____

_____

_____

_____

_____

_____

_____

_____

_____

_____

_____

_____

_____

_____

_____

_____

_____

_____

_____

_____

_____

_____

_____

_____

_____

_____

_____

_____

_____

_____

_____

_____

_____

_____

_____

_____

_____

_____

CHAPTER 5

Curfews

If you ever want to see the differences in parenting styles of your friends and family, ask when they put their kids to bed at different core ages. We can all agree that proper sleep is one of the most important factors in raising children. Not only is sleep developmentally important, and a crucial touchstone in the routine that children crave, but as they get older, proper sleep helps maturing children make better decisions. It creates a solid stability that enables them to stay out of trouble throughout the day. Better than that, it helps during the most important time when lapses of judgment commonly occur, past normal bedtimes in the wee hours of the morning.

My boys constantly reminded me that they were the only ones who had such a thing as a "curfew." As a parent, I would always inwardly scoff, knowing that many of those "friends" my kids spoke of definitely had a curfew and my sons were being lied to. It was "uncool" to be required to be home by a certain time, and I heard about it on many occasions.

In high school this curfew was a strict 10:00 p.m. on weekdays. My husband and I understood the necessity of giving them freedom, so on weekends the boys were allowed a little extra leeway according to their high school grade level. These numbers may look different in your house. Every decade of growth in our world creates a new paradigm for child rearing. These were our markers to ensure we provided freedom and stability for growing (what we believed) would be responsible humans. Boys growing into men that understood the *why* behind our curfews helped them *appreciate* those extended weekend times.

Our home curfews were:

- Freshman: 10:00 p.m.

- Sophomore: 10:30 p.m.

- Junior: 11:00 p.m.

- Senior: midnight

Remember those hockey players we hosted in our home? Our rules were a standard for our home. If you were staying within our walls, the rules applied to you, not just to our sons. That meant our hockey players had to follow those same curfew rules. You might think it silly to impose house rules on children that don't belong to you, but they were in our charge. It was our responsibility to keep them safe and that meant that we would love them and treat them with the same parental guidance that we did our own sons. Curfew applied to all in our home, but one thing any parent knows about rules is that sooner or later, one of your kids, whether biological or not, is going to break one.

One night, two players staying with us thought they would sneak out after curfew. It is always funny to me when kids think they are silent in their escape. If only they had known, I heard them climb out the basement window and venture off. I checked each room for evidence of escape, and to this day, I chuckle when I think about it. One had stuffed all his clean (or dirty) clothes under the comforter to look like he was sleeping with his hat strategically placed, and his earphones on a basketball. It was a very creative effort, while the other merely left the light on and the door open. While in the basement, I closed and locked the window and headed upstairs to nap on the sofa. I made sure when they arrived and learned their entrance was no longer their saving grace, they would have only one way back in: Through the front door where I was lying in wait to hear the creative explanations that only kids caught in the act can come up with. Each attempted to sneak in past the sofa. As they nearly made it past, I chimed, "Have a good time?" One scoffed at being caught and the other sung like a canary.

They both quickly learned the consequences of sneaking out and making poor choices. How? With a break-of-dawn run. This moment showed me clearly the importance of keeping curfews clear. There is nothing that scared me, and many parents, more than knowing a child may sneak out and your next moment of contact could be a call in the middle of the night. Either from your child, or from the local police letting you know something tragic has happened. I never wanted to get that call. I knew there was a level of parental responsibility to preventing it, so this rule became one that created a safety net, not only for our three sons, but for all the children that would filter through our home over the years.

Independence is something you build. It isn't something that just happens because you are on the cusp of adulthood. Starting with Christmas break of senior year, we removed curfews, along with other house rules, so that the boys could practice independent responsibility. We wanted them to be given a chance to make good and bad choices while still under our safety net. Better to have poor choices made when parents are present to talk through how to reach better outcomes.

Curfews

Investigate with your children about the pros and cons of curfews. You may find that engaging in a discussion, rather than operating from the strong arm, gives you a chance to share your perspective and gives them a chance to offer their input so they feel heard.

Do you think that your children could benefit from a curfew? How do you think you could begin this important conversation?

_____

_____

_____

_____

_____

_____

_____

_____

_____

Your Notes

_____

_____

_____

_____

_____

_____

_____

_____

_____

_____

_____

_____

_____

_____

_____

_____

_____

_____

_____

_____

_____

_____

_____

_____

_____

_____

_____

_____

_____

_____

_____

_____

_____

_____

_____

_____

_____

_____

_____

_____

CHAPTER 6

Cooking and Meal Planning

" Give a man a fish, and you can feed him for a day. Teach a man to fish, and you will feed him for a lifetime." Clichés are useful for a reason. They contain tidbits of truth that, like all things, serve to bring us to realization of a lesson. The lesson here is the worthwhile skill and investment of teaching your children to cook.

There are so many lessons that go beyond the financial—and hopefully—culinary benefits of eating home-cooked meals. What happens when you create a space where the meal becomes a daily family event? When you have each person contributing it gives you a chance to build life skills and positive relationship experiences for your family that will become cherished memories. Much has been written about the important grounding point of family meals, proving another notion about the family who eats together.

We made use of summers during the middle school years to provide many opportunities for life lessons and skills. One of our main focuses was on cooking and meal planning on a budget. That first summer, the boys were responsible for planning three meals a day for a month. To make it more fun, we turned it into a contest. Whoever could create the best meal with their allotted funds would win. The boys scoured the newspaper ads to assemble the best meal for the lowest price.

I remember one such meal where the boys were each given $10 and sent to the store to find dinner for the family. So many lessons come without planning for them. The unintended extra lesson of teamwork yielded a dinner of ribs, canned corn, oranges, and milk from their pooled funds.

To quote yet another saying we like to use in our family, "Failing to plan is planning to fail." I found it exceedingly helpful to schedule family meals a month at a time in one-week blocks. Since most lunches were at school or work, we planned breakfast and dinner. For example:

Monday

Breakfast	Egg bake
Dinner	Soup

Tuesday

Breakfast   Berry, chocolate, and lemon poppy
             seed muffins
Dinner   Pasta night

Wednesday

Breakfast   Waffles with ham slices
Dinner   Take-out pizza

Thursday

Breakfast   Dinosaur egg oatmeal
Dinner   Slow-cooker meal

Friday

Breakfast   Scrambled eggs and cheese
Dinner   Left overs

Saturday

Breakfast   Cinnamon rolls or monkey bread
Dinner   Casserole night

Sunday

Breakfast   Bacon and pancakes
Lunch   Take-out Chinese
Dinner   Cheeseburgers, chili fries, and
             chocolate milk shakes

As you can see, this was an entirely manageable planning schedule with a fair amount of variety. I recall at least one time that my boys did not appreciate the effort. One of the easiest lessons we will be given the chance to teach, is the one of gratitude. Complaints about privilege are easier to manage when you nip them from the start.

One morning I heard one of my boys say, "Ugh, *this* again for breakfast." Naturally, I couldn't let the teachable moment pass. The next day breakfast was a nutritious bowl of Kashi cereal. From the way they all reacted, you would have thought I had killed them. One of the boys said it tasted like a cow had already eaten the cereal and left it for him to eat again. I knew it was a good opportunity to teach them not to complain about meals that not only were cooked for them, but also served to them. I went about my morning, keeping a neutral stance on their seemingly endless complaining until it was time to take them to school. When I returned, I found cereal in the trash and sink disposal. Sometimes the easy lesson is one that takes the longest to cement into the mind.

Wastefulness was one of those hard lessons I would not allow to pass without full comprehension. To make my point, I promptly bought a month's supply of cereal and watched closely to see that none of it went to waste. After the first day the boys couldn't wait for their old breakfast routine, but they had to tough it out for the month. This occurred during the ten-year stretch when we were billet parents for sixteen- to twenty-one-year-old hockey players. Whenever they or our own boys broke the rules, all were deemed *guilty by association.* Our dear hockey player also enjoyed a month of cold cereal. After a month of easy breakfasts, I heard far less complaining about the repetitive nature of my homemade hot breakfasts.

What are some of the lessons you have/want to teach your children about food, money, and the value of gratitude when being served?

_____

_____

_____

_____

_____

_____

_____

_____

_____

_____

_____

_____

_____

_____

_____

_____

_____

_____

_____

_____

_____

_____

_____

_____

_____

_____

_____

_____

_____

_____

_____

_____

Your Notes

_____

_____

_____

_____

_____

_____

_____

_____

_____

_____

_____

_____

_____

_____

_____

_____

_____

_____

_____

_____

_____

_____

CHAPTER 7

Summers

Summer is classically when kids spend their time goofing off and potentially getting into trouble. We knew from our own experiences that trouble happens when the mind and hands are lacking in something to do. We worked hard to make sure that all their time was structured. To that end, starting in middle school, during the summer, our boys were required to have some sort of job. Even if they had an activity such as a sport or a theatrical production to keep them busy, we felt it was important that they fill the extra time with some sort of work, even if that meant work around the house.

This wasn't a punishment. You may think it was a bit harsh of us to require some level of responsible work to be had. Instead, it was meant to develop responsibility within each of them and made sure that "idle hands" were not in a position to get into mischief. With the amount of time that kids have during their summers to get bored, we knew the best way to keep the boys out of trouble was to keep them busy. Not just busy for the sake of busy, but busy with a greater purpose to build well-rounded humans.

During high school summers, the boys took at least one college class and worked twenty hours a week. When summer classes were out, they had to work forty hours a week. You might scoff at the strict rules we had in place. My husband and I carefully considered each of the reasons why we built our rules this way. It was about helping our boys understand that someday these great responsibilities would not just be a partnership they had with us, but something they would be required to do on their own.

We continued the practice even after they became full-time college students. We wanted our boys to have as much of our help as possible to create the best educational and financial outcome for their future, so we committed to supporting their adult goals. Education, whether trade school or a four-year college, would be provided for them at our expense, so that we could best equip them for adulthood. Our boys knew that we were in the fortunate position of being able to help in their college education. Many of their friends did not have the same opportunity to have their time in college paid for, so they had a great appreciation for what we were providing. That said, they would always take summer classes as a way to avoid a very expensive fifth year of education.

Part of how we made sure the importance of education was understood was in the often-outdoor labor jobs we would find for them to do in the summer. It not only provided a steady reminder of the long-term health benefits of working hard, but also how their future could look different with a good education. We wanted to make sure during those impressionable years, that our boys had many opportunities to understand how their lives might be different with the choices they made for their futures.

All their jobs paid well, but at the end of the day they were exhausted. As you can expect, my sons sometimes complained to others of their overly busy summer schedules and lack of free time. In the end, each of them has shared with me how they came to appreciate the work and the life lessons that work conveyed.

Do you know what your children want to be when they grow up? Have those important and deep conversations and make sure that you equip them with the resources you do have. You don't have to pay for college to know you have given your best with the most important lessons about building responsibility within your kids.

What are some of the most important lessons you want to instill in your children before they venture off into adulthood? How can you better equip them today?

_____

_____

_____

_____

_____

_____

_____

_____

_____

_____

_____

_____

_____

_____

_____

_____

_____

_____

_____

_____

_____

_____

_____

_____

_____

_____

_____

_____

_____

_____

_____

_____

_____

CHAPTER 8

The Ball that Bounces

What do you think is the most important responsibility you have in this life? I am sure you have heard many different ideas about what the most important aspects of life are. When I think about work and family, the idea of juggling the many things that life places in our hands can be overwhelming. How do we know what we need to be focused on?

One example that has brought an interesting perspective on the juggling of life's balls is from author Nora Roberts. Jennifer Lynn Barnes shared on twitter, her experience at a Q & A with her.

Roberts was asked how to balance writing and kids, and she said, "The key to juggling is to know that some of the balls you have in the air are made of plastic, and some are made of glass. If you drop a plastic ball, it bounces, no harm done. If you drop a glass ball, it shatters. You have to know which balls are glass and which are plastic and prioritize catching the glass ones."

Roberts was not talking about juggling five balls. She was talking about juggling *fifty-five* balls. The balls don't represent "family" or "work." There are separate balls for everything that goes into each of those categories. "Deadline on Project Y" or "Crazy sock day at school." Her point, addressing a room full of women, was not "prioritize kids over work." It was "some kid stuff is glass and some is plastic, and sometimes, to catch a glass work ball, you have to drop a plastic family one, and that is okay." And the reverse is also true. Sometimes, to catch a glass kid ball, something at work has to slide, and that is okay too. If you are juggling fifty-five balls, some are going to drop, so you have to focus not on broad categories, but on the glass balls."

Remember this, importance is an opinion. If you ask your friends with kids what is more important, work or their kids' events, you will get a mixed response. Some will say work because that is what supports those activities. Some will say the memory of watching their kid play and the knowing they didn't miss the game. The big difference in opinion comes when you ask the person it impacts the most. Your kids. Talking with your kids about the things in life that they think are important will give you a better idea of what balls they have that are glass or plastic. The same goes for you sharing with them about the things that are important to you. You will give them a deeper understanding into your everyday life and your candor will help them grasp some of the hardest topics that life has to bring.

What are some of your own "opinions" on what is important? How do you think bringing your spouse and kids into the discussion would change the way you see and juggle those glass and plastic balls?

_____

_____

_____

_____

_____

_____

_____

_____

_____

_____

_____

_____

_____

_____

_____

_____

_____

_____

_____

_____

_____

_____

_____

_____

_____

_____

Your Notes

_____

_____

_____

_____

_____

_____

_____

_____

_____

_____

_____

_____

_____

_____

_____

_____

_____

_____

_____

_____

CHAPTER 9

Financial Management

If there is a lesson that will help your children see success in life, it truly lies in their understanding of money. Financial stability can make those plastic and glass balls we discussed before even easier to juggle. We encouraged our boys to understand that avoiding debt and the chaotic situations that lead to it is the crucial first step. Our boys were taught to avoid debt from an early age.

We learned important lessons from Dave Ramsey so we could not only be able to teach our boys about money, but be good stewards with what we had. My husband and I wanted to be the foundation for our boys. When you build on a solid foundation, the storms of life that will surely come don't destroy what you have built.

Investing

Do you think your financial future would look different if you had the chance to invest before adulthood? While we didn't have these kinds of opportunities, we wanted to provide this learning opportunity for our boys.

We showed them how to invest $2,000 a year from the ages of nineteen to twenty-six (*it's just a cup of coffee a day*). By doing this they would have disposable income later. This wasn't just so they would have funds available for a rainy day. This was to teach them the value of small steps. If they saved a little now, they would increase the likelihood that they could enjoy life later when retirement arrives and you don't want to continue being career-focused. We also encouraged them to have emergency funds. We shared that *they* are responsible for their life—nobody else is. We taught them not to depend on others when they retire, to see to it that they have more than enough for their lives.

Oftentimes, we think of our legacy that is passed on to the next generation in terms of financial endowment. There is nothing wrong with creating and sharing a financial legacy; it can be a well-appreciated gift. In my mind, there are other and more valuable gifts that we can give to our children. Lessons of love, memories, and knowledge are gifts that will stay with them long after financial support has been spent. Thinking back, I remember the great gifts my mother and father gave me in the secrets of living well—without leaving behind great financial wealth.

I tried to do the same for my own sons. Often when they would go to bed, my husband and I, exhausted, would sit down and talk about the budget we had created. How would we get through until the next week? Sometimes it would cause us to rub two pennies together, and yes, there were some occasions where we would often have heated arguments. I have gratitude in knowing that we learned quickly what really is important.

Competing with the Joneses and buying our sons a brand-new car equipped with leather seats, payments, and interest wasn't going to help us or them achieve the goals for college. So, what did we do? We would buy a well-loved used car that we could pay for with cash. By not being bogged down by a car payment, we created the space for us to create more savings for our boys. When you want to provide as much financial help as you can, don't be afraid to sacrifice the flashy driving symbol for the lesson in gratitude. Not just for a car that comes without payments, but for the ability to give our kids the chance to be kids for just a little while longer. All the while helping provide a stable future for them to start their adulthood without tens of thousands to hundreds of thousands of dollars in college debt.

When they wanted to spend their money on something, they had to save up the amount to buy it. This habit increased the value of things they did purchase and discouraged frivolous spending. During their senior year, we also required them to pay for their cell phones and car insurance. We wanted them to practice budgeting. We wanted there to be a clear understanding in the difference between how to make ends meet and what it meant if paying bills equaled going without the latest and greatest shiny object.

We are firm believers in Dave Ramsey's common sense methods for achieving financial peace of mind. We encouraged our boys to begin investing as soon as they started to work. The compounded interest from investing just $2,000 per year from the early-life ages of nineteen to thirty-six will yield great dividends later in life, especially if a person continues to invest until retirement. Not only will such early practices give kids financial security as they approach mid-life, but it will create more opportunities for enjoyment in later life when they have accumulated disposable income to spend on vacations, spouses, and grandchildren.

I highly recommend taking a Dave Ramsey course and commit yourself to learning more about money. If this isn't something you have personally made a reality, don't worry! It isn't too late! No matter where the start on your road to financial freedom is, the first step is always the hardest. One of the most important things we did was to build emergency accounts to avoid being financially fragile when the unavoidable uncertainties in life were encountered.

If starting from scratch, the first saving goal should be an emergency fund for small crises like car trouble. This will provide a pillow of security as other financial challenges like debt are handled. As little as $1,500 will give security for most everyday problems. The second goal is a fund that would cover all expenses for six months in case of a major crisis such as being laid off from a job.

We are responsible for our lives. While there are ways to survive your retirement on what the government offers, you shouldn't depend on that. You have the power and the responsibility to create the kind of life that you want when your working days have reached their end. The power of foresight and good spending habits will greatly increase the possibility of accumulating more than enough personal wealth to cover expenses for the rest of one's life.

Do you have a savings or college plan for your children? If you don't, it is never too late to start. Remember, even if you only have a small amount to give, anything that you have for them when it's time for them to spread their wings will give them an advantage in life that many others don't get. You have the power to make that choice and that change in your financial life.

What is one thing you could do
to help feel more prepared for
when your kids go to college?

_____

_____

_____

_____

_____

_____

_____

_____

_____

_____

_____

_____

_____

_____

_____

_____

_____

_____

_____

_____

_____

_____

_____

_____

_____

_____

_____

_____

_____

_____

_____

_____

_____

_____

_____

_____

_____

_____

CHAPTER 10

Traditions

What traditions did you grow up with? Some of those may still bring a smile to your face or a mild cringe at the thought, but no matter what your response is, it likely brings to mind time spent with family. Those traditions were meant to create a lasting memory or impact on a moment. We can all agree that kids grow up fast, but at the time it doesn't always feel like it.

There were many family traditions that I brought from my own upbringing and added to. I created a number of monthly traditions to mark the passage of time. Each one created to build lasting memories, and sometimes just to keep my boys busy. Boys aren't necessarily the most craft friendly, and truth be told, the very mention of craft projects often made my boys edge toward the door, especially as they got older. The best part was knowing that once they actually got started, my kids enjoyed the stability of these traditions.

Planned activities such as these not only created a dependable opportunity for family bonding time, but they also produced childhood creations that I cherished immediately. These creations have been saved not only to show me the time that has passed, but to share these things with my boys and their families—something they can cherish and remind them of these times we shared. Some of the projects included stepping-stones, Christmas ornaments, and thumbprint art, to name a few. These are things that any parent can do. It isn't necessary to create a giant, extravagant project that will overwhelm you and create more chaos than fun. The goal is to find simple and easy things to do when your kids are young; keep it simple and fun. Attention spans, which are short when they are young, don't get all that much longer when they are older; they just have different distractions.

You don't have to reinvent the wheel in order to create traditions for your family. There are numerous resources available from which to gather ideas to establish these traditions. Tools, such as Pinterest, have made it even easier to find creative projects. Here are some of the monthly activities and traditions we participated in with our boys over the years. You don't have to use anything that I have listed, this is just to share with you how simple some things can be to create. You don't have to make anything fancy. A simple notes file on your phone can suffice as a way for you to keep track of the things you want to do and capture with your own family. Remember, the best way to create a tradition is to get everyone involved!

January:

- Reading books aloud while sipping homemade hot chocolate.

- Sledding with the boys and coming home tired and cold to a warm slow-cooked meal.

February:

- Reading Dr. Seuss's *Green Eggs and Ham* aloud while eating green eggs and ham at breakfast.

- Reading about Abraham Lincoln on Presidents' Day while eating Lincoln Logs (jelly rolls).

- Make a trail of Hershey's chocolate kisses from their rooms to the breakfast table on St. Valentine's Day. Cupid "shoots an arrow" into the morning milk, which would magically turn pink with red food coloring.

- On George Washington's birthday, eat cherry pie and learn lessons from his life.

- Share the great classic movies with our kids, like *Casablanca.* There is usually a good lesson to be drawn from the positive and negative characters of great movies, such as how to be an honorable man, or how to treat women with dignity and respect.

March:
- St. Patrick's Day: the morning milk would turn green after a visit from Lewy the Leprechaun. Dinner would consist of either Irish stew and soda bread, or corned beef, cabbage, and potatoes. In the evening we would watch a classic romance, *The Quiet Man.* The boys seemed to like the trout fishing and the fight scenes the best.

April:
- Whether Easter fell in March or April, we would leave a trail of candy eggs from the boys' bedrooms to the breakfast table, where a light breakfast would hold them until after church. Then we would begin the afternoon with a wonderful lunch, followed by an Easter egg hunt.

May:

- On May Day, we decorated an angel food cake with white and blue frosting for dessert. Then we would make "fishing poles" out of those long pixie sticks, and long licorice with a bag of "caught" goldfish crackers hanging from the end.

- Go to the cemetery to place flowers on the graves of all our relatives and tell the boys stories about their ancestors and what they did in life.

- The baseball season would begin, so there were often games to attend. Even on the other nights, we would play catch and get exercise chasing wild throws.

- For Mother's Day, my husband always made sure there were homemade cards, breakfast, and gifts.

June:

- On Sundays, bike to the lake with a picnic breakfast of coffee cake or muffins, fruit, and juice. Prepare the food the night before so we would be ready to go in the morning.

- On Father's Day we would make Dad breakfast in bed, and when my boys were younger, they would crawl in with him and eat all of his bacon.

- We would make fresh strawberry shortcake and spend the evening together watching *The Sound of Music.*

July:
- Blueberry and strawberry pancakes with whipped cream to celebrate America's independence.

- Attending summer parades, and taking picnics to listen to the bands that played in the park.

- Refreshing the artificial flowers at the cemetery to remind our sons to respect and honor those who have gone before us.

August:
- Mounting the chalkboard in the kitchen with a yellow school bus would mark the start of back-to-school month. Prior to the actual start of class, the boys would begin preparing for their new schedule by going to bed earlier, while the summer sun was still above the horizon.

- Toward the end of summer, we would do cookouts at a nearby park with grills, roasting hot dogs on sticks and cooking beans in their cans over the coals. After the boys had run off most of the meal, we would make s'mores with raspberries, which were messy and delicious.

September:

- Family biking continued as fall sports began: first football, then hockey. I have found that well-exercised boys are the happiest.

- Meals in the slow-cooker and soups on the stove were warm and easy meals. Everyone looked forward to the seasonal return of fresh, warm pumpkin bread.

October:

- Chili joined the list of soups, along with fall vegetables and squash.

- Early in the month we would make luscious caramel apples covered with candies, then later in the month we would carve pumpkins. We learned early to always buy a couple extra, not only because carving mistakes would inevitably happen, but also the extra seeds were a wonderful toasted snack.

- "The Great Pumpkin" visited on Halloween to turn the breakfast milk and scrambled eggs orange. Before bed, we always enjoyed watching *It's the Great Pumpkin, Charlie Brown.*

November:

- Corn candies and salted peanuts were a common munchable decoration in our house in November.

- Our family would volunteer at the local community center for a Thanksgiving Meal to serve others. Most years we were given the job of delivering those meals to people who could not leave their homes. This was a great opportunity to teach our sons about generosity as well as thankfulness. When we finished, we would return home for our own Thanksgiving meal, and take turns sharing the things we were thankful for and the different blessings we each had throughout the year.

December:

- Christmas movies were a staple throughout the month of December, especially *It's a Wonderful Life* and *Miracle on 34th Street*.

- We would wrap gifts with a local charity organization in our town for families in need. It was a beautiful reminder for my boys of the importance of doing for others who may not have the same things that they did.

- We would go to Church on Christmas Eve, and the boys would find an elf's sack on the front porch when we returned. This "magic" was achieved with the help of a friendly neighbor.

- We would drag out our sleeping bags and sleep near the fireplace and Christmas tree, waiting in hopes of catching sight of Santa Claus on Christmas Eve. One of my fondest Christmas memories is my youngest son asking me to dance whenever "Christmas Shoes" came on the radio. He couldn't have realized it at the time, but it was my favorite yearly Christmas gift, and the song still warms my heart when I hear it.

- The lesson of giving was one we truly wanted to impress on our boys. So, Christmas morning started with us sharing those gifts we wrapped with those who needed them. We were fortunate enough to be able to hand deliver the gifts to those families. Once we handed out the gifts, we went home to celebrate Christmas and open presents together. So many lessons were learned from the simple act of giving.

What are some of your most cherished traditions? Create a list of the ones you have and consider if you want to create new memories and new traditions that your own children can pass on to their littles.

_____

_____

_____

_____

_____

_____

_____

_____

_____

_____

_____

_____

_____

_____

_____

_____

_____

_____

_____

_____

_____

_____

_____

_____

_____

_____

_____

_____

_____

_____

_____

_____

_____

_____

_____

_____

_____

_____

_____

CHAPTER 11

Birthdays

Celebrations big and small are exciting for children. I think we can all agree that for most any child, the biggest yearly landmark, outside of Christmas or the beginning of summer, is their birthday. If we are honest, there is something exciting about celebrating another year while those who love you seek to shower you with love and of course, presents.

As most parents, we always tried to make birthdays special for our boys. When they woke up and came to breakfast, there would be a big "Happy Birthday" banner, a cover for their chair to make it look like a throne, and a special plate and cup with their name on it. Until they were thirteen, the special breakfast of choice was donuts with chocolate milk and juice. Still, despite their increasing age, they anticipated each year when they would be raised up and celebrated.

Birthday Traditions

Ages 1–5 years

Nearly every parent has a collection of cheesy art drawings and handprints to mark the ages. This became a birthday staple to mark their growth. Between the ages of one and five, we helped the boys make T-shirts with their age, handprints, and footprints painted on them. It has been fun for me to reflect back on how little they were and how much they have grown since those days. Knowing how special these items are to me, it might even be a fun gift for their spouses someday.

Ages 6–9 years

Once your child is of school age, you arrive at the dreaded class birthdays. Some of the parties we hosted through the years included baseball, whiffle ball, and a fishing theme with bowls of goldfish as party favors. One year, we had a pirate theme, where we buried "treasure" and gave the boys a map to find it. Remember that these parties are not about extravagance, but about creating the space to make memories that will last you and your children a lifetime.

13 Years

We would talk to the boys about their dreams and what they wanted their future to look like. We asked them if they wanted to attend college or trade schools to aid them in reaching the goals, they saw for themselves. You may think this is a bit early, but we wanted them to think about these things so that when the time came to choose, it didn't feel like we were throwing them into a frozen lake and expecting them to claw their way out.

16 Years

As one of the biggest youthful birthday milestones, we sought to make sixteen extra special. For their sixteenth birthday, we gave them sixteen small gifts emphasizing the transition to this big year! The actual day of celebration would begin with the traditional donuts for breakfast, followed by the newly qualified driver piloting their siblings to school in the family car. Sometime during the day, we would show up at the school with a used car—covered with sixteen balloons—that they could call their own.

Among gifts of treats and clothes, they would receive a page of old sayings and pearls of wisdom that they could reference in the future; a pertinent Ann Landers article; a sports blanket made from their old sports shirts, of which they had accumulated many by this time; and the book *Have a Little Faith* by Mitch Albom (of Tuesdays with Morrie fame). Other gifts included a domino set of their own (since they all grew up playing dominoes with their grandfather), and a safety kit for their car, complete with a snow shovel, toolset, and safe winter driving information. The last gift was the movie *Stand by Me*, which is a family favorite, and one that impresses some incredible lessons about friendship that we felt were priceless for this time in their lives.

17 Years

As kids get older, helping them understand how money works becomes a big focus. When ours arrived at their seventeenth birthday, we gave them each a credit card with a $200 limit and told them not to use it unless they had the money to pay for it. We also included with that the understanding that if you *can* pay for it, then you shouldn't use a credit card anyway.

21 Years

For their twenty-first birthday, each boy received a two-day Vegas vacation with a friend. Dad went along as a chaperone to steer them away from any serious trouble but still afforded them the grown-up freedom we knew they wanted to be shown. The birthday boy would be given $200 to have fun for the two-day trip. They were told that once that money was gone, it was gone. Our oldest son was way up in the first hour and thought he would move to Vegas to make his millions, but by the third hour he had lost all of his winnings and most of the money we had given him, with still six hours of evening to burn. Vegas is not a fun town if you don't have money, and he couldn't wait to leave. He and his friend found a bar with cheap drinks, crawled back into the hotel room in the early morning, and got just two hours of sleep before they were due at the airport. The second important lesson of the trip was that flying sleep-deprived and severely hung-over is miserable!

I would like to say my younger sons did better, but despite the foreknowledge, the other boys had similar experiences. None of them have shown any interest in returning to Vegas or gambling in general, and that is good for a mother's heart for sure!

After 21

As a parent, one of the hardest things you will ever let go of are the traditions you built to create memories and experiences for your children. Adulthood means that you give up those parts of their lives as they build new traditions with their friends and a family they work to build on their own. Birthdays become more about spending time together and much less about the gifts. In today's world, that quality time together may be harder to achieve in person but may be accomplished (if need be) with a little face time.

Walking through the ways we celebrated birthdays may seem flawless and ready to be a sizzle reel on social media. The truth is, there were many rough years with birthdays that were smaller or heavier because life happens. The way that we made these traditions work was by being intentional and determining how and when we wanted to make an impact on those pivotal ages. It isn't a perfect formula. For us, this helped keep things memorable and gave our boys the opportunities we believed would create the most significant impression on their growing hearts and minds.

How can you make upcoming birthdays a way to create special memories?

_____

_____

_____

_____

_____

_____

_____

_____

_____

_____

_____

_____

_____

_____

_____

_____

_____

_____

_____

_____

_____

_____

_____

_____

_____

_____

_____

CHAPTER 12

Graduation: The First Serious Good-Bye

Nothing can prepare you for the first good-byes you experience as a parent. From the first day dropping them off at school, to the day they leave home, our hearts are never ready to let go of what God has entrusted to us for nearly a quarter of a century. While it may seem trivial that preschool or kindergarten would bring tears, each moment where you as a parent are charged with letting go a little more is tough and you must give yourself the space to feel and grow through it. I promise you, honoring your feelings as you learn to say good-bye throughout your child's life is how you will survive it.

Depending on the age of your children, you may have already taken the first one to school for that first day. I don't know about you, but I cried in the parking lot after putting on a brave face as they found their way to a desk with their name on it. You are going to face many good-byes as a parent, from first chaperone-less field trips, mission trips, and sleepovers. Your responses to these pivotal moments of independence all lead up to the first serious good-bye you will face as your child leaves behind childhood to embrace adulthood.

Graduation from high school is the biggest good-bye in the parent-child relationship. Up to that point, you have been gradually increasing their independent responsibility in small increments. Starting with their first steps and increasing in ownership of responsibility like learning to drive. When a child leaves the house for college or trade school, they begin to take on more adult responsibility, further removed from a parent's safety net of influence and guidance. It is something that can be scary, but if you create another memorable experience, you can make another positive mark on their lives.

To mark the occasion, and to provide them with some small symbolic reminders, I gave my sons the practical gift of a suitcase with these messages inside:

- A lemon. When life gives you lemons, make lemonade.

- A deck of cards. You can't control the hand that is dealt to you, but you can learn to play the game.

- A pair of kid's jeans. Everybody puts their pants on one leg at a time; don't let others intimidate or control you.

- A small boot. When things turn unfavorable, pull up your bootstraps and keep going.

- A pencil. Pencils have erasers; use them and learn from your mistakes.

- The children's book *The Lion and the Mouse.* Even the smallest and weakest can help you, and you can help them: Don't be arrogant or selfish.

This was huge for me as I know my husband and I had worked very hard preparing our sons for this day of launching from home. However, this brought me to my knees seeing the bags packed and the backside of my sons taking off on the next chapter of the lives they are now writing. Between pain and sheer happiness hitting myself with tears of sorrow and joy, I knew my job of mom was changing in a way that would never return to what I knew, ending my time as protector and moving me into the position of spectator.

My advice to you as a parent: You will never be ready for them to fly from your nest, so prepare the best you can.

What tools can you prepare to send off with your children when the time comes for this good-bye?

_____

_____

_____

_____

_____

_____

_____

_____

_____

_____

_____

_____

_____

_____

_____

_____

_____

_____

CHAPTER 13

Engagements: The Second Good-Bye

More good-byes? I wish I could say that the college good-bye is the last one you will need to endure, but we know that the other significant farewell is when your child leaves your family to start their own. While you can't choose your children's spouses, you ought to give them the tools to make this very important decision wisely.

As our sons have approached marriage, we have been careful to impress upon them the gravity of the decision. It is no surprise that a good marriage can be the cornerstone of a wonderful adulthood and a fruitful life. Sadly, a bad marriage can be a compounding source of stress and hardship leading to difficult experiences and unfortunate decisions. Marriage isn't just deciding to love someone for the rest of your life. It is a choice to be part of something that is bigger than just you.

When you decide to pair your life up with someone else, it is very important to take the best version of yourself into a marriage. If you don't love and respect yourself, how will you expect someone else to? You also need to choose someone who not only will help you continue to grow, but whom you can help continue to grow in kind. Marriage is not a destination, but a decision of love and sacrifice that starts a journey that, if done right, through hardship and happiness, will flourish and sustain both you and the person you have chosen to bind yourself to.

Here are the five guidelines we suggested to our boys on the subject of marriage. These aren't fool proof by any means, but for us, we wanted to make sure that we equipped them for their future spouse with love and intention.

1. Consider waiting until the age of twenty-five before marriage so that you have the freedom to see the world and expand your perspectives. Plus, your frontal cortex is fully developed and you have a better chance of choosing with more than just emotions. You will have logic on your side as well.

2. Build a strong faith and be open with your partner early in a relationship regarding your expectations

if you want to marry and start a family. The person you want to spend the rest of your life with should know how you feel about important life issues, about your faith, and about the things that you believe in. When they don't know those things before you get married, you set yourself up for unknown quantities of conflict that could have been avoided by being honest in the beginning.

3. Date people with lives and interests outside the relationship. Neither you nor your parent should be responsible for the other person's entertainment and happiness. If your partner has worked to get a degree and they want to pursue those things, make sure you support that.

4. Don't start an engagement or a marriage with debt. Buy a ring you can afford or pay it off before you propose.

5. A little financial security will go a long way early in a marriage. While it may never build a family beyond their spouse, security can be built by taking the average family of four and using that number to build a six-month emergency fund before the wedding.

Before our boys proposed, we encouraged our sons to write a resolution that they can give to their future bride detailing the man they are, the man they want to be, and what they wish to bring to the marriage. As a way to encourage our sons to see what we saw in each of them, we also wrote a letter to our sons reminding them of the roles they will be taking on by beginning a family, of the men we knew they were already, and how much we believed in them to be the men their new family would need.

We have advised our sons that another major consideration when choosing a marriage partner should be the fiancée's extended family. It is an unavoidable fact that when someone marries, they form an attachment to a whole family, not just one person. A spouse's family may have an enormous influence on the couple's life and marriage, both positively and negatively.

It might also be highly informative to observe an intended fiancée's parents: people tend to become their parents as they age. At the very least, those personality traits the parents exhibited in their formative years will be the default inclination when those children start their own families, which might be a help or a hindrance to them. We told our boys that it was wise to observe a girlfriend's mother, because the girlfriend may become her mother someday.

What are some of the ways you can encourage your children to build a strong family before they begin the journey to creating one?

_____

_____

_____

_____

_____

_____

_____

_____

_____

_____

_____

_____

_____

_____

_____

_____

_____

_____

_____

_____

CHAPTER 14

Weddings, Gifts, and Second Motherhood

Though much of the same advice in the previous chapter would apply to daughters as well as sons, there are some traditions that apply exclusively to daughters. Since God gave me sons instead of daughters, some of those traditions had to be modified for my future daughters that came through my sons getting married.

For example, I didn't have a daughter to whom I could offer my wedding dress. Since offering my dress to a not yet daughter-in-law, I sought to create a way to give a small gift from something that meant the world to me. Since I wanted to contribute something personal, I asked my future daughter-in-law if a ring pillow made from my wedding gown. I have kept the remaining part of my dress and plan to have those pieces integrated into the seamed edges of crocheted blankets, which will be given as christening gifts should we be blessed with grandchildren. I mentioned this before, but it is worthwhile to share it again. When you become a parent, things change. No matter how you become a parent, whether through pregnancy or adoption, your life becomes a journey of raising someone who can build their own family someday. Their wedding day belongs to them, but there are so many ways you can help create special and memorable moments with your children and their soon to be spouse.

Another way we sought to include our soon to be daughters into our family was a pre-wedding gift. The night before the wedding, we gave our future daughter-in-law a strand of pearls along with a letter welcoming her into our family. The pearls are the strand that will tie our family to the daughter we never had and tie us all together as a family. Joining two families together is tough and it was our goal to make sure that the person our son was joining lives with knew we were committed to this new part of our family.

Another one of our gifts to the couple was an Irish crystal bell. This isn't so they could summon each other during times of sickness, though it could certainly do the job. The intended use of this bell, instead, is this: When conflict occurs in the marriage, whether the disagreement is large or small, ringing the bell is an opportunity to call a timeout, take a breath, and hug to take the edge off the fight. Stopping to process a moment can help to put the conflict in perspective. It can give proper pause for considering the love and sacrifice that are part of marriage. Such a device can be a useful deterrent to unintended words that might escape at the height of a passionate argument. The light touch on a crystal bell and the dainty sound can help de-escalate an argument before it gets out of control. Think of it like a softer version of a boxing-match bell. Even accidentally breaking the bell in a too-aggressive ring can be a deterrent; it's a reminder of what can happen emotionally if we don't put conflict in its correct perspective.

What are some of the techniques you have used to de-escalate fights and problems and how can you share those tools with your children to help them find their way through conflict in their own relationships?

_____

_____

_____

_____

_____

_____

_____

_____

_____

_____

_____

_____

_____

_____

_____

_____

_____

_____

_____

_____

_____

_____

_____

_____

_____

_____

_____

_____

_____

_____

_____

_____

_____

_____

CHAPTER 15

Faith

Each of us has a different thought process when it comes to faith. Some of us find ourselves anchored into a faith we grew up in and some of us find out faith along the way. You may be someone that has yet to find out what that word means for them, and that is okay! This life is a faith journey of its own, and it will be something that you find you learn along the way. That is when you will begin to create faith moments you share with your children.

For me, faith is an integral part of my life. I want to share this with you, not as a means to convert you, but to show you how faith is something more than just a building where people go on Sunday. Faith begins before we are born. It is a journey here on earth and it is when your life here ends and you go home for eternity. Faith is the belief in a Creator, one who is our heavenly Father, and the understanding that He placed you on earth at this specific moment in time to do His work through you. "Before I formed you in the womb, I knew you, before you were born, I set you apart" (Jer. 1:5 NIV).

We live in a world that goes by themes like "dog eat dog" and "every man for himself," but faith gives you a chance to be here on earth and think of others first. The way that you give back and serve, and the hard work and strong moral ethics you choose to live by, will shape not only you, but others who are around you. When it is time to step over the threshold of this life into forever, there is only one sentence we want to hear: "Well done, good and faithful servant." (Matt. 25:21 ESV)

It isn't always easy to know what the right decision is. Sometimes we think we know, and it may be that we find out later that the morally grey area was darker or lighter than we thought. When you use your faith as a compass, you can stand fast in knowing you have a much better success rate in finding the right road to travel on. While many times there will be pain in the decisions that we make, and we do not always understand the pain it may bring, we can be steadfast knowing that God can use the pain to propel us forward because it is for the greater good.

Every life journey is different. We are not meant to see all of the journey God has set before us, though our faith should take us in His direction, even if we find ourselves getting there by a different path than others. A huge lesson in life is that of failure. We are not always going to make the right decision. Sometimes, rather than be guided by our faith, we will be propelled into chaos by our feelings. When this happens—and it will—you have to make the choice to give yourself forgiveness so that you can get back on the right path.

I am not saying that this is easy. In fact, it is the opposite. The easiest path is the one of least resistance. Many of us have learned that we can get that brief hit of bliss from the things of this world. It is easier to chase after the instant happiness that you feel by changing direction for a shiny object than facing some of the hard thing's life throws at you. The problem with this quick change is that it's only an illusion. Material things, once obtained, quickly lose their effectiveness at keeping us happy.

You can play with it, boast about it, and show it off to others hoping it will place you in a position to believe that good feelings come from objects and the approval of others and not from within ourselves. Trying to find something that brings that same feeling back that your old shiny object once had becomes a never-ending cycle of materialism that traps you on a treadmill with no end to seeking out that next happy thing. The truth of trying to gather more and more things is that it won't bring you the sustained happiness you are looking for. We know many people who have less and are happier because they don't live in an expectation of getting the next big thing. When you remove the ability to get things on demand, it creates a simplicity that many of us wish we could master.

The bigger truth about faith is that happiness is not the goal. Joy is sustainable and happiness is a momentary feeling. We all should seek joy from simple things like family, God, and a job well done.

For my family, faith is something that is foundational. We see things differently whenever we look at where God has been left out of raising our children. Kneeling at the bedside has been replaced by hasty prayers said as covers are pulled close to chins. Work floods our schedule and church comes too early on Sunday mornings causing us to watch it online, listen to the radio, or skip it altogether. Many families no longer gather together for a meal around their own kitchen table because sporting events, long workdays, and drowning schedules in children's activities have taken priority.

It isn't an impossible thing to change. We can all make sure that we create the priorities we want our children to embrace into adulthood. The key is that *we* get to choose what those things are. If it is important to you to share these things with your children, then begin now.

When I felt the world trying to force its way into my home, I turned off the TV and knelt with my children by their beds and said prayers with them. I took them to church on Sunday mornings and made a game out of how their lives could be like those that were talked about in service. This alone helped my boys begin to listen to the messages being shared during service.

No matter where you eat, pray, and love, remember that it is always a good time to teach gratitude and prayer. And it is always a good time to help your children see how much different the world looks through the lens of faith.

What are some of the faith traditions that you share with your family?

_____

_____

_____

_____

_____

_____

_____

_____

_____

_____

_____

_____

_____

_____

_____

_____

_____

_____

_____

_____

_____

_____

_____

_____

_____

_____

_____

_____

_____

_____

_____

_____

_____

_____

_____

_____

_____

_____

_____

_____

_____

_____

_____

_____

_____

_____

CHAPTER 16

Perennial Reminders

There are so many different ways that you can share the holidays with your family. There is also something that matters to each of us and that is how we share real life reminders throughout the year. As we begin to near the end of our time together, I want to share with you some of the ways that I celebrate different times in our lives, and what those "reminders" have looked like for us. I always believed tangible and visual items were the best instruments to have around as they represent the possibilities one can achieve

A star; Thankfulness; always keep your head up, watching for your shooting star, and don't lose sight of how lucky you are in life.

An arrow; Honesty; always "shoot straight" with people.

Dreamcatchers; Remember to follow your dreams.

Some of the other symbolic gifts that we gave to our boys when they were children were:

- Yellow pencils in a jar reminded them that just as you can correct a mistake with an eraser when writing, there is no error in life that you cannot begin to fix if you try.

- A letter written by their grandparents to keep, which will serve as a way to have a piece of their grandparents' own thoughts with them, even after their grandmas and grandpas have passed on.

- A skeleton key, to remind them that locked doors require special tools: If they are curious and diligent, they can overcome the barriers in their lives.

- A compass, to remind the boys to find the True North of their lives.

Whatever your inspirational objects are, and no matter what phrases you use to bring awareness of the never-ending life lessons we all face, remember that these reminders stick with your kids better than you think, and when you choose to create these anchors for them to remember, you are equipping them **far** beyond the moment. You are giving them space **to** learn and imprint these words and concepts on **their** hearts and minds. That, my friend, is priceless.

What are some of your favorite inspirational phrases or images that help you stay on course and want to instill within your own family?

_____

_____

_____

_____

_____

_____

_____

_____

_____

_____

_____

_____

_____

_____

_____

_____

_____

_____

_____

_____

_____

_____

_____

_____

_____

_____

_____

_____

_____

_____

Your Notes

_____

_____

_____

_____

_____

_____

_____

_____

_____

_____

_____

_____

_____

_____

_____

_____

_____

_____

CHAPTER 17

Mom's Simple Rules

Throughout the lessons, rules, expectations, and foundational principles that we used to parent our children, I have asked you to think inwardly about your own parenting journey. Dig deep into those questions that I shared with you and create the traditions, the foundations, and the faith that you want your family to grow with. Knowing how you want them to look back at their lives as they grow forward is a gift you give to them that keeps on giving long after they no longer live under your roof.

Thank you for being part of this journey with me. Our children are the greatest investment we will ever make in this world, and the impact they have is directly related to the effort and time we put into helping shape them into adults that will change the world. Before I leave you to go forth to create your own memories and traditions, I want to share with you my basic rules as we both continue this journey as parents.

"Let everything you do and say be governed by Mom's rules":

Be gentle and kind - You never know what is happening in someone else's life.

Be simple in your tastes and sincere in your ways – Complicated needs and wants is where things begin their path to creating chaos in your life.

Do your best – Failure only matters if you quit.

Have fun – Life is meant to be enjoyed through all the many emotions and moments it shares.

Be safe – You can change more lives and enjoy your time with your loved ones even more if you are still here on this earth to be a part of it.

I am hopeful that I have provided useful lessons to my boys as they begin their own families. At the time of this writing, I had yet to make the third promotion of motherhood into being a grandparent. While I don't know if grandchildren are part of God's plan for my life, just in case, I have gathered a collection of children's books to share. This book was created for my boys to be a reference guide to begin building some of the traditions that I know are part of who they are today.

Our time together has come to an end, and I am so grateful that you have come alongside me to be part of this journey. My hope is that you feel inspired to make your own rules and traditions that will build lasting impressions and create memories that are shared through generations. You are smarter and stronger than you think. Whether you are a mom, a dad, a grandparent, a foster parent, a caregiver, or even just a friend, you can make the world better by just being you. The world needs you and I am grateful, that for just a moment, we shared this story together.

Cheers!

Gratitude

How do you thank everyone that helped you create your legacy? You do your best.

To my heavenly Creator, thank you for the family you gave me to, the lessons I learned and the salvation you bring. It all started with you.

All my thanks and love to my parents. You both are one of the most amazing blessings and gifts in my life. Your grounded nature taught me more than you could ever realize. You were my guiding light and the central pillar that held me up in all the good and bad times. You both instilled in me (and my siblings) the essential elements of what family should be. You both did it with such a never-ending love and supportive approach. Caring in action. Dad, you were a craftsman who taught us to put care into all of our work. When you care, everything and everyone matters. You said, "You must care about crafting the back of the fence as much as the front. Why? Somebody will see it and they will know." (Love, Justmee)

To my siblings, thank you for helping me choose the best of our parent's teachings and showing me what family truly means. You never failed to remind me that since I was the youngest, when I needed new tires, mom and dad just got me new used car.

My sons, watching you grow in life is my greatest joy. Seeing how these life lessons have created strong, respectful, and brilliant young men brings such light into this mom's world. Through each of your examples as grown men, you motivate me every day to be a better mom and role model. I wanted to leave you something that would last forever. I wanted to leave you a tangible keepsake of the lessons that we learned together, side by side. When I thought about what that looked like, no shiny object seemed to serve that purpose. I pray my legacy can continue to make an impact on your lives. Every word printed on these pages only exists because of you, my sons. I couldn't have made this journey without you. I hope that I have left a positive thumbprint on all three of you. (LYM)

To my amazing assistant writer, Tiarra at The Legacy Architect, who accepted a random book introduction to me from my publisher. You were generous and gracious with your time, advice and guidance. Thank you. To Shane at Carpenter's Son, thank you for believing in my book enough to publish it and put it out in the world.

To you, my reader, for picking this book up and maybe even learning a few things from this seasoned mom.

Lastly, I give eternal gratitude to and for my husband, whose love is my life's compass. Thank you for your endless love and support. Thank you for your inner strength that inspires me every day and thank you for our sons. Forever and two days.

About the Author

Author and Mentor, **Kim Sorensen** started her career off as first a wife and then a mother. After her own upbringing inspired her to create a framework of lessons and traditions, she raised up 3 successful boys and began looking for a way to create more impact as an empty nester. Through mentorship in local churches and leadership in women's groups, Sorensen takes those lessons learned as a mother and helps others not only build their faith but encourages them to leave their own mark on their families. With her boys grown and creating families of their own, Sorensen is dedicated to serving, teaching and growing within her church and community.

You can learn more about Kim and the tips and tricks she used raising her boys on her website at: www.GiftsAndSecretsBook.com